THE FOREST FEAST
gatherings

Simple Vegetarian Menus
for Hosting Friends & Family

Erin Gleeson

Abrams
New York

Published in 2016 by Abrams
An imprint of ABRAMS

Photography, recipes, illustrations, food styling, and text by
Erin Gleeson © Copyright 2016 Erin Gleeson/Forest Feast, LLC.
Photo on page 3 by Nicole Thompson. Photos on pages 16 and 215
(lower right) by Marc Lipovsky. Photos on pages 22 (top left), 132
(lower right), and 250 by Jonathan Prosnit. Photo on page 196 (top
left) by David Tsay, reprinted with permission from *Better Homes
and Gardens*® magazine, ©2015 David Tsay, All rights reserved.
Recipes on pages 44, 54, 102, and 210 are adapted from bhg.com.

Library of Congress Control Number: 2015955670

ISBN: 978-1-4197-2245-5

Editor: Laura Dozier
Designer: Erin Gleeson with Liam Flanagan
Production Manager: Denise LaCongo

The text of this book was composed
in Traveling Typewriter and
author's handwriting.

Printed and bound in China

10 9 8 7 6 5 4 3 2 1

Abrams books are available at special
discounts when purchased in quantity
for premiums and promotions as well
as fundraising or educational use.
Special editions can also be created
to specification. For details, contact
specialsales@abramsbooks.com or the
address below.

ABRAMS The Art of Books
115 West 18th Street, New York, NY 10011
abramsbooks.com

For Jonathan

contents

introduction

It's hard to believe it's been four years since we moved from New York City to the woods. In 2011, right before we got married, Jonathan and I left Brooklyn because he was offered a job in the Bay Area, not far from where I grew up. After studying photography, I had been working as a professional food photographer in New York for several years—and heading west meant starting over in a way. By chance we ended up finding a cabin in the northern Santa Cruz Mountains that felt rural but was an easy enough commute for Jonathan. I planned to work from home, and at the time I had no idea that this unique place would shape my work in a completely new way.

The light is so amazing here—foggy mornings and golden afternoon light make it a fantastic place to shoot outdoors. When we first arrived in California, I started a blog called *The Forest Feast* (www.theforestfeast.com) as a motivation to make new work. I started posting photos, along with some of my watercolors (which I'd only ever done as a hobby). Before I knew it, people began noticing, and within a year I was lucky enough to have a contract to create my first cookbook, *The Forest Feast*—a total dream project. I joke that the book was my first baby, since it took me about nine months to create. But shortly after the book came out in 2014, our beautiful baby boy, Ezra, arrived and made our little home in the woods feel even more special.

Jonathan and I have always done a lot of entertaining, and I've been working on easy party recipes for years. We host a lot of Friday night Shabbat dinners and weekend cocktail parties for friends. We both come from families that love to cook and have people over, and we feel it's important to bring people together in our home around food. For me, the whole process of preparing the meal and the ambience is a creative outlet—I think of it as one big art project, which I enjoy making and curating. It's a nice gift to your friends and family.

Anyone can entertain—it's fun and rewarding. Nevertheless, as much as I try to prepare ahead, I am often running around trying to pick up the house or blow-dry my hair right before guests are supposed to arrive. (I love a guest who arrives fashionably late!) I've had plenty of practice, but even I get overwhelmed sometimes, so I completely understand why people get stressed and even want to avoid entertaining entirely. However, there are so many ways to make it manageable—and most important, enjoyable. Over the years I've discovered a lot of memorable recipes and learned a lot of shortcuts, tips, and tricks, so it made sense for me to focus my second cookbook on such an important aspect of my life—gathering friends and family together to share a festive meal.

With this book, I hope to make entertaining approachable and fun. I offer ideas on how to keep things simple so that you can not only enjoy preparing for the party, but also enjoy your guests and the food. Even when I lived in a small apartment in New York, I adapted my space so I could host friends, which usually meant a standing cocktail party as opposed to a sit-down dinner. Having people over is a valuable relationship (and hence community) builder. Your home offers a unique view into your world, which helps people understand you more intimately. Similarly, cooking with local produce helps you connect with the place that you live. Sometimes I simply run to the grocery store, but when I can, I try to buy and cook fresh, local produce as I think eating food grown nearby and meeting the farmer who grew it creates a meaningful connection and supports my community.

Sometimes the hardest part is deciding what to serve—what goes together, what's seasonal, what can be made ahead, suits the occasion, and accommodates guests' food restrictions. So, this book includes a series of tried-and-tested vegetarian menus that I hope will make the whole process easier. Because I am a home cook, my recipes are simple. Local produce in our weekly farm box is usually my starting point, and I like to really highlight the flavors of each vegetable, often just by using a little olive oil and salt. And because of my background in art, I aim for recipes that are colorful. This is the mentality that informs my entertaining advice and the kinds of recipes that I share in this book—food that is impressive enough for a party but easy enough to whip together after a long day of work.

In each menu, I offer guidance on preparing, serving, and displaying the food and drink. I've also included some general entertaining advice, with ideas for décor, flower arrangements, and buffet labels. The menus serve six to eight people unless otherwise noted and generally include a drink, appetizer, salad, side, main, and dessert. I intend for them to be served casually, either on a buffet table or passed around the table family-style. I also make suggestions along the way as to what can be done in advance and what to do first. And even though the recipes in this book are geared for entertaining, each recipe can stand on its own if you need a quick salad or a weeknight dinner idea for a smaller group. Just halve the recipe, and it will serve three to four people.

Preparation time has been carefully considered in the menus in this book. I usually do the shopping and some prep the day before, but I do most of the cooking the day of. Depending on the occasion, Jonathan and I don't have more than a few hours to get everything ready on the day of the party. So, when compiling these menus, I tried to design a series of recipes that could be made by two people in less than three hours, especially if you've prepped a few things ahead that I have suggested. Some menus are more ambitious, including six items (like my seasonal feast menus, which I imagine one might host on a Saturday evening), while others are a bit shorter, like my Weeknight Gathering menu (page 217).

There are a few essentials that are almost always present when I entertain, which I do not list in each menu. In addition to a cocktail, I also usually offer beer, wine, juice, and/or seltzer, and I put salt, pepper, bread, butter, and a pitcher of water on the table.

If you're low on time, you can simplify the menus further. Skip the cocktail and just serve beer and/or wine. For the appetizer, serve bowls of nuts and olives instead. Ask a guest to bring dessert, or serve store-bought chocolates and cookies. That leaves you with just the meal items to prepare (salad, side, main). You can also assign recipes to friends and turn a menu into a potluck!

There are lots of other ways to streamline your efforts. For instance, I always make sure to have a detailed to-do list for the day of. I also write out the menu and keep it in the kitchen so that I don't forget any courses in the fridge (which has happened!). Jonathan and I have our party-prep routine down like a well-choreographed dance! We confirm the menu together the day before, and I do the grocery shopping. We cook together, but if we BBQ, he does that entirely. The morning of, we talk about where the tables and chairs and bar will be (usually outside) and he sets all of that up while I cook. We usually have one buffet table, one bar table, and a couple groupings of chairs where people can sit. He sets the tables and I add finishing touches like flowers and candles. When guests arrive, Jonathan offers them a drink while I finish up the food. I make it a point to leave the kitchen when guests arrive so I can have a cocktail with everyone and make them feel welcome before it's time to pull dinner out.

Ambience is very important—especially lighting and music. Don't skip this, and try to have it set before guests arrive. I like low lighting when entertaining in the evening. A string of twinkle lights and a couple votives can make a world of difference! And it's important to have music on before your guests arrive. Music can fill in the gaps on any awkward silence during conversation if guests don't know each other.

I've thought a lot about what my goal is with *The Forest Feast*, and I think it all comes down to creating community through healthy food. There's a unique opportunity to create relationships and friendships when entertaining in one's home. We try to be thoughtful with our guest lists and think about which people would enjoy meeting each other. While the food might be the centerpiece to a dinner, conversation is just as important, and asking a shy guest a question about what they've been working on might be all you need to do to get them talking (offering a cocktail helps, too!). At Friday night dinners, Jonathan's family has a tradition of going around the table and sharing the best part of their week, which I think is a great way to settle guests into the dinner table and get conversation started.

Entertaining is half about the preparation and half about the actual party—and getting ready should be fun. Have your to-do list on the counter, your apron tied, and your music on! Pour yourself a glass of wine and have fun cooking with a friend or family member. This will put you in a great mood for when guests arrive, and the rest will be a piece of cake. Guests will remember the vibe and conversation more than details like the centerpiece or whether or not you had a specialty cocktail. Remember that everything doesn't need to be perfect; enjoy your company—after all, that's what it's all about.

Happy hosting!

Erin

tips for using this book

MEASUREMENTS

T	tablespoon
t	teaspoon
c	cup
kg	kilogram
g	gram
cm	centimeter
mm	millimeter
in	inch
L	liter
ml	milliliter

MY FAVORITE salad dressing
¾ c olive oil
¼ c balsamic vinegar
2 T soy sauce
2 T sesame oil

shake in a jar

GARLIC

I often use garlic powder because it's quick, but you can always substitute real garlic. Use about 1 clove per ¼ t.

SALT { When I mention salt, I always use coarse or Kosher salt when cooking & flaky Maldon sea salt to finish.

If a recipe calls for scallions, chop the whole thing (white & green parts).

✳{ Simplify any menu by serving wine instead of the cocktail, nuts & cheese in place of the appetizer & store-bought chocolates or cookies for dessert. Then you'll just have to make the side & main dishes. }✳

set the mood

It's a good idea to create the ambience before guests arrive. That way, if you're running around at the last minute trying to finish things up (as I often am!), guests walk into a welcoming environment. Even if the food isn't done, I make sure to light candles, arrange the flowers, put drinks and glasses out so guests can help themselves, and play some music (usually old jazz or Spanish guitar without lyrics so it's easy to talk over). I also always make myself a list with the menu plus a list of things to do last minute. If I'm running behind, I like to leave a few things that are easy for people to help with, such as opening bottles of wine or slicing bread.

MENU
summer rolls - appetizer
panzanella
farro salad
portabellos
pineapple - dessert

TO DO
cut the bread
boil the farro
roast the mushroom
slice the pineapple

spring feast

menu serves 6-8

DO AHEAD: The night before, mix the punch (but add flowers & seltzer just before serving), grate the radishes & grate the cheese for the pizza (or just buy already grated) & slice the strawberries for the dessert. A couple hours ahead, toast the baguette for the Radish Butter Crostini & prep the pizza. I usually bake the pizza right as guests arrive.

SERVING SUGGESTIONS: Serve the punch & crostini to start & put all other items on a buffet. If you're low on time, serve white wine instead of the punch, radishes & butter instead of the crostini & skip the Parmesan Snap Peas.

picking wild mustard in the spring in nearby Pescadero, CA

GROW YOUR OWN EDIBLE FLOWERS!
....
nasturtiums are easy to grow in pots & provide colorful blooms for salads

FLORAL/EDIBLE TABLE RUNNER

Gather greenery off nearby trees & bushes (or buy greens & ferns from a florist) to create a centerpiece runner down the middle of your table without using vases. Scatter a mixture of small, colorful fruits, vegetables & flowers over the greenery. Here, I used mini eggplants, halved limes, kumquats & shortly trimmed carnations. Other ideas include apples, pears, plums, citrus, small peppers & artichokes.

Intersperse candles in mason jars throughout. Choose flowers that do well out of water like carnations, orchids, calla lilies, sunflowers & mums.

23

Floral Punch

* 1 T rosewater
* 4 c (960 ml) pink (or strawberry) lemonade
* 4 c (960 ml) seltzer
* 1 c (240 ml) gin

Combine all ingredients in a small punch bowl or large mixing bowl with ice & floating edible flowers

You can mix the punch the night before, but leave the flowers & seltzer out until just before serving. Serve with a ladle & extra flowers for garnish. Rosewater has a unique, strong, floral flavor & can be found at Middle Eastern grocery stores or gourmet shops. Look for pesticide-free edible flowers like violas, rosebuds, calendulas, carnations, nasturtiums & marigolds at the farmers' market, in gourmet shops, or online. If you can't find flowers, garnish with fresh raspberries or lemon slices.

RADISH BUTTER CROSTINI

① GRATE
6-8 radishes
(leave tops on to make it easier; can be done the day before)

② MIX
grated radishes with ¼ c (55g) butter
(butter should be very soft, almost melting)

③ SPREAD
radish butter on slices of toasted baguette
(you'll need about ½ of a baguette; toasting can be done ahead)

SPRINKLE WITH COARSE OR FLAKY SALT LIKE MALDON →

HERB SALAD

← 1 head butter lettuce
(torn into pieces)

1 c (40 g) basil leaves →
(loosely packed)

½ c (25 g) mint leaves
(loosely packed)

½ c (25g) chopped cilantro →
(leaves & stems, loosely packed)

½ c (25g) parsley leaves
(loosely packed)

¼ c (15g) chopped dill
(loosely packed)

Toss all ingredients in a bowl & dress just before serving
with your favorite vinaigrette (see page 16 for mine)
or simply olive oil, lemon juice & salt.

PARMESAN Snap peas

TOSS IN A BOWL:

* 4 c (240 g) snap peas
  (ends trimmed)
* ½ c (50 g) grated Parmesan
* ½ c (50 g) breadcrumbs
* 2 T olive oil

Lay the mixture out on a baking sheet

SPRINKLE WITH:

(a pinch each)
* salt
* pepper
* cayenne
* garlic powder

BAKE at 425°F (220°C) 15-20 min

Enjoy warm or at room temp. The mixture can be prepped several
hours ahead but it's best baked within an hour of serving.

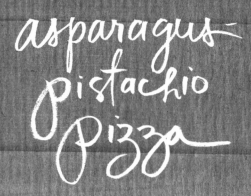

asparagus-pistachio pizza

makes 2 small pizzas
(8-12 slices)

YOU'LL NEED:

* 2 (16-oz/455-g) packages pizza dough
* 4 cloves garlic, minced
* 3 c (330 g) grated mozzarella
* 1 bunch asparagus (about 40 stalks)
* ½ c (50 g) grated Parmesan
* ¼ c (30 g) chopped pistachio nuts

(buy grated cheese or grate it the day before)

Roll each piece of dough out to about
12 in (30.5 cm) & place on an oiled baking
sheet. First spread olive oil over the
dough, then sprinkle with garlic &
mozzarella. Next trim asparagus to about
6 in (15 cm) long, slicing any thick
stalks in half lengthwise. Lay out the
asparagus in a radiating pattern over the
cheese. Sprinkle Parmesan & pistachios over
the asparagus. Drizzle each pizza with
olive oil, salt & pepper before baking.

Bake at 425°F (220°C) for 20 min

(or follow the dough's package instructions)

I prefer this pizza right out of the oven, but you can make it up
to 1 day ahead & reheat. Each pizza provides 4-6 slices,
making 2 pizzas just about right for a group of 8;
halve this recipe for a smaller group.

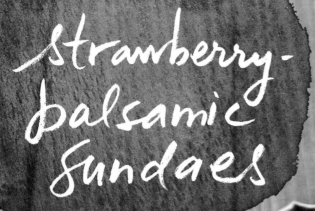

strawberry-
balsamic
sundaes

top 2 scoops
vanilla ice cream
with:

1 t best-quality balsamic vinegar

2-3 sliced strawberries
(can be sliced the day before)

enjoy immediately!

For 8 people, you'll need about
2 pints (946 ml) of ice cream &
a small carton of strawberries.
I like to set out a bowl of sliced
strawberries & let guests make
their own sundaes.

Wine + Cheese Party

menu serves 10–12

DO AHEAD: The night before, cut or grate the cheeses for each recipe, plus slice the watermelon & nectarines. Store all items separately in the fridge. The cheese ball can be made the day before & rolled in the nut mixture a couple hours before serving (make the nut mixture ahead). The Zucchini Flatbread can be assembled &/or baked a few hours in advance.

SERVING SUGGESTIONS: These wines are best enjoyed in the order above. I like to set one bottle of each wine next to the appropriate appetizer on a table with small signs. It's fun to go down the line & try each pairing with guests as a group. I suggest pouring each person about 2 oz (60 ml) of each wine per appetizer. This menu is meant to be enjoyed as a cocktail party & can be served with crudités on the side & chocolates to finish. You can simplify this menu by just sampling 3 wines: a prosecco, a white & a red (in that order).

make signs to
label each wine
& cheese using
clementines or
any other fruit
(see page 182)

prosecco & camembert

SALTED NECTARINE TOASTS

1 baguette or French bread loaf

3 nectarines (white or yellow)

8 oz (225g) Camembert cheese

Cut the bread & lay the pieces out on a baking sheet.
Top each with a small wedge of cheese a couple thin
slices of nectarine & a drizzle of olive oil.
(If nectarines are out of season, try pears or Fuyu
persimmons. Cheese & fruit can be sliced ahead.) Broil
on high for 2-3 min, or until golden & melted. Best hot,
but also good at room temperature. Before serving,
drizzle with more olive oil & flaky salt (like Maldon).

enjoy with a cold glass of Prosecco

pinot grigio + parmesan

ZUCCHINI FLATBREAD

16 oz (455g) pizza dough

roll into a large, thin rectangular
shape, brush with olive oil & lay out
on a greased baking sheet

2 zucchini

make ribbons from the zucchini
using a peeler & lay them out on the
dough in stripes, overlapping a bit

1 c (100g) grated Parmesan

sprinkle the Parmesan over the zucchini

2 chopped scallions
1 T pinenuts

sprinkle on top

BAKE at 425°F (220°C) for 18 min or until golden

Slice into strips & serve warm or prepare ahead & serve
at room temp. Enjoy with a glass of Pinot Grigio.

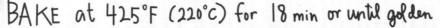

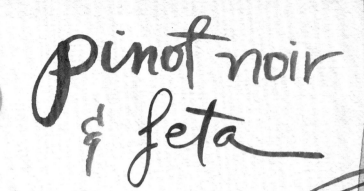

pinot noir & feta

WATERMELON-FETA BITES

- 1 small seedless watermelon
- 8 oz (225g) feta
- 1 bunch mint

Cut the watermelon into
1-in (2.5-cm) cubes & the feta
into ½-in (12-mm) cubes
(can be done ahead).
Stack on a toothpick
with a mint leaf on top.
Serving suggestion:
2-3 bites per person.

enjoy with a
glass of Pinot Noir

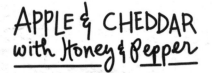

APPLE & CHEDDAR
with Honey & Pepper

3 very round apples (Fuji works well)
8 oz (225 g) sharp white Cheddar
2 T honey
freshly ground black pepper

Slice ¼-in (6-mm) rounds off the sides
of each apple (if done ahead, brush lightly
with lemon juice to keep from browning).
Cut the cheese into ¼-in (6-mm) thick squares
(can be done the day before). Arrange the apple
rounds on a platter & place one cheese slice
on top of each. Drizzle honey & sprinkle black
pepper over all. Serving suggestion: 2 per person.

enjoy with a
glass of Cabernet

port & gorgonzola

BLUE CHEESE BALL

- 8 oz (225g) cream cheese
- 6 oz (170g) crumbled Gorgonzola
- 5 chopped scallions

mix well by hand &
roll into a ball
(can be done the day before)

enjoy with a glass of Port

salad buffet

menu serves 6-8

DO AHEAD: All of the food can be made ahead & served at room temperature. Make the Apple Matchstick Salad last to avoid browning. You can chop the carrots & cucumbers the night before, as well as make the quinoa. The sangria, except for the mint, can be made several hours ahead. The zucchini and the watermelon balls are best prepared up to only a couple hours in advance.

SERVING SUGGESTIONS: Place all the salads on a buffet table for guests to serve themselves. I like to also serve a nice rustic loaf of French bread with butter or cheese alongside these salads. If you're low on time, serve white wine instead of sangria & skip the Apple Matchstick Salad.

FLORAL ARRANGEMENT
in a bowl

Create a beautiful floral
arrangement simply using tape &
a bowl. Any size bowl works! Just
attach the tape across the top of
the bowl in a lattice pattern & fill
it halfway with water. I buy a few
different types of flowers, like
carnations & peonies, that are a
similar color (in this case, pink) &
mix them with greens I pick outside.
Place stems through the holes to
create a low arrangement that's easy
to see over on the dining table.

① →

② →

③ Cut stems short & group types of flowers together instead of interspersing them.

④ Have greens spilling out of one side of the bowl to make it feel a bit wild. I like to use fresh herbs like rosemary, thyme, or mint, plus foraged leaves, branches & vines.

⑤ Place the bowl on a plate or platter to create a table centerpiece.

CUCUMBER-MELON
sangria

½ honeydew melon,
seeded & cubed

1 cucumber,
thinly sliced

1 lime, thinly sliced

1 c (50g) mint leaves,
loosely packed

ml) bottles of
several hours

zucchini "noodle" salad

← 3 large raw zucchini
(the fatter the better)

← 1½ c (280g) edamame
(I buy a bag of shelled, precooked beans)

← 8oz (225g) ciliegine
(mini fresh mozzarella balls)

← 4oz (115g) pine nuts
(sunflower seeds also work)

6 oz (180ml) pesto →
(store-bought)

Use a spiralizer to make "noodles" from the zucchini.
Toss in a bowl with all other ingredients. Serve chilled or at room
temperature. Best made no more than 2 hours before serving.

Moroccan Carrot Salad

5 med carrots
(sliced into thin "coins" using a mandoline or knife)

½ c (100g) cooked quinoa
(about ¼ c dry, cooked according to package instructions)

⅓ c (50g) golden raisins

⅓ c (45g) pepitas
(shelled pumpkin seeds)

½ c (75g) chickpeas
(I use canned & drain them)

**3 T {parsley (flat leaf)
each {mint**
(fresh & chopped)

DRESSING

1 T apple cider vinegar
1 T maple syrup
¼ t cumin
3 T olive oil

Toss all ingredients. This can be made ahead but add pepitas, herbs & dressing just before serving. The quinoa can be made the day before.

apple
MATCHSTICK SALAD

¾ c (90 g)
chopped pecans

4 apples
chopped into
matchstick-size
slices

½ c (15 g) cilantro, chopped
(leaves & stems)

½ c (73 g)
dried cranberries
or raisins

toss all ingredients with olive oil, lemon & salt

ARTICHOKE-POTATO SALAD

ROAST about 3 lb (1.4 kg) mini
red potatoes (halved) &
15 whole cloves garlic
with olive oil, salt & pepper
at 450°F (230°C) for 25 min.

(or until tender + golden)
This can be done the day before.

TOSS cooled potatoes &
garlic with 16 oz (455 g)
sliced marinated
artichoke hearts &
3 oz (85 g/about 2 big
handfuls) arugula.

*dress with your
favorite vinaigrette*
(or mine on page 16)

can a be served warm, but toss with
a ri efore serving to minimize wilting

watermelon-tomato salad

3 T chopped
basil

balls from
1 small seedless
Watermelon
(can be done ahead)

3 T chopped
mint

3 T chopped
cilantro

1½ c (220 g)
yellow cherry
tomatoes

2 T crumbled **feta**

Mix the watermelon, herbs & tomatoes &
lay out on a platter. Sprinkle
the top with feta, olive oil & salt.

iced tea party

menu serves 6-8

DO AHEAD: The teas (without any mint or fruit) can be made the night before and refrigerated. The eggs can be boiled, peeled & halved the night before (or simply buy hard-boiled eggs). Make the filling for the deviled eggs & keep it in the fridge overnight; spoon it into eggs up to an hour before serving. Prep the strawberries for the kebabs & the vegetables for the tea sandwiches the night before & keep them in the fridge. The shortbread can be made the day before.

SERVING SUGGESTIONS: Serve everything at once on a buffet table. The shortbread is meant for dessert. If you're low on time, just make 2 types of iced tea, skip the Strawberry Caprese Kebabs & serve store-bought shortbread cookies for dessert.

*Each tea recipe makes eight 8-oz (240-ml) servings. For a smaller group, you can halve the recipes. All can be made the day before & garnished just before serving.

berry iced tea

Boil 4 c (960 ml) water & pour into a pitcher with 8 berry-flavored tea bags. Let steep for 10 minutes, then remove tea bags & add 4 c (960 ml) cold water, plus enough ice to fill the pitcher. Add ⅓ c (40 g) fresh raspberries & fresh blackberries to the pitcher. Serve tea in glasses filled with ice.

green-mint iced tea

Boil 4 c (960 ml) water & pour into a pitcher with 4 mint tea bags & 4 green tea bags. Let steep for 10 minutes, then remove tea bags & add 4 c (960 ml) cold water, plus enough ice to fill the pitcher. Add 3 fresh mint sprigs to the pitcher. Serve tea in glasses filled with ice.

orange iced tea

Boil 4 c (960 ml) water & pour into a pitcher with 8 orange-flavored tea bags. Let steep for 10 minutes, then remove tea bags & add 4 c (960 ml) cold water, plus enough ice to fill the pitcher. Add slices from 1 orange to the pitcher. Serve tea in glasses filled with ice.

* agave syrup can be served on the side & is great for sweetening iced tea

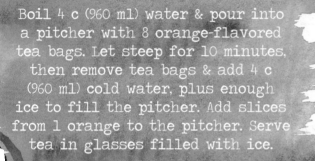

lemon iced tea

Boil 4 c (960 ml) water & pour into a pitcher with 8 lemon-flavored tea bags. Let steep for 10 minutes, then remove tea bags & add 4 c (960 ml) cold water, plus enough ice to fill the pitcher. Serve tea in wide-mouthed glasses or jars with lemon ice cubes.

freeze lemon slices & water in cupcake tins to make lemon ice cubes (fill with water about halfway)

69

TEA SANDWICHES

You'll need 12 slices of bread and about 8 oz (225 g) of cream cheese to make enough for 8 guests to each have 3 triangle sandwiches.

① Spread 1T cream cheese (room temp) on each slice of bread

② very thinly slice in long strips or circles:
- •5 RADISHES
- •1 YELLOW SQUASH →
- •1 ENGLISH CUCUMBER
  (I use a mandoline)

③ Alternating ingredients, lay the sliced, raw vegetables over the cream cheese layer to cover the bread completely. Using a large chef's knife, slice off crusts, including flaps of vegetables hanging off the edges. Then slice each open-faced sandwich in half diagonally, creating triangles. Garnish each triangle with a sprig of dill, then sprinkle with olive oil, flaky salt & pepper before serving.

DILL →

*Tip
The vegetables can be sliced & stored in the refrigerator night. Sand- wiches e asse h

Hummus-Tomato Deviled Eggs

① Peel & halve 12 hard-boiled eggs then remove & set aside yolks

② Mash yolks in a bowl with:

2 T hummus
2 T mayonnaise
2 T mustard

(can be mixed the day before)

③ Spoon mixture into egg white halves

garnish each with a grape tomato half,
plus a sprinkle of paprika & salt

strawberry caprese kebabs

1 STRAWBERRY
1 BASIL LEAF
1 MOZZARELLA BALL

} stack on a short kebab stick

(trim strawberry tops)

drizzle with olive oil,
salt & pepper before serving

serving suggestion:
3 kebabs per person

↓

for 8 servings (24 kebabs), you'll
need 24 small/med strawberries,
1 bunch of basil & about 16 oz
(455 g) mini mozzarella balls

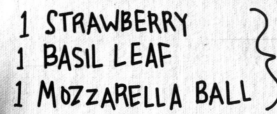

BLACK-PEPPER shortbread

⅔ c (135g) sugar
1 c (225g) salted butter
2 c (250g) flour
1½ t black pepper

Briefly pulse all the ingredients in a food processor until combined. Firmly press the crumbly mixture into a 7 by 10-in (17 by 25-cm) baking dish & bake at 325°F (165°C) for 30 min, or until the edges are slightly golden. Cool 5 min, then cut into 2-in (5-cm) squares. Allow to cool completely before removing squares from dish. Can be made the day before or a few weeks ahead & frozen.

FRESHLY GROUND

summer
FEAST

menu serves 6-8

DO AHEAD: The watermelon, peaches, tomatoes & pineapple can be sliced or chopped the day before & stored in the fridge. The summer roll dip, the undressed panzanella & farro salad, the vinaigrettes for the panzanella & farro salad & the chimichurri can all be made the day before. The bread for the panzanella can be toasted the morning of.

SERVING SUGGESTIONS: The summer rolls can be served as an appetizer or with the meal. Everything is great at room temp (except the portobellos, which should be served warm). Place all dishes on a buffet so guests can serve themselves, except for the pineapple, which I put out later for dessert.

watermelon-mint water

at a warm outdoor gathering, I've noticed guests often just want water. I like to add cubed seedless watermelon & sprigs of fresh mint to a dispenser or pitcher of water for a fresh, colorful twist.

Other herb-infused water ideas:

cucumber - rosemary
strawberry - basil
blackberry - thyme
lemon - cilantro

The water can be prepared up to 2 hours in advance (the fruit can be chopped the day before). Chill if you have room, otherwise add ice before serving, or serve alongside an ice bucket.

Floral Summer Rolls

TIP

I like to soak rice paper
wraps one at a time in a
large skillet of cold water.
Soak one while you wrap
another. Place pretty items,
like flowers, down first,
so that they show once it's
rolled up & tuck the end
flap underneath so it doesn't
cover up the flowers. Fold
it like a burrito, as tightly
as possible. Look for edible
flowers at the farmers'
market, gourmet grocery
stores, or order them
online. See pages 22 & 24
for suggested types
of edible flowers.

fill round rice paper wraps with some or all of these ingredients:

- fresh herbs, like basil & cilantro
- fresh edible flowers, like nasturtium & viola
- romaine lettuce leaves
- red onion, thinly sliced into rounds
- avocado, thinly sliced
- carrot, grated or peeled into ribbons
- scallions, sliced in long strips or chopped
- cucumber, cut into thin spears or rounds

serving suggestion:
2 rolls per person

DIP: equal parts soy sauce, olive oil &
sesame oil (can be made the day before)

Peach Panzanella

Cut 1 crusty baguette or half of a rustic French loaf
into 1-in (2.5-cm) cubes. Lay out on a baking sheet &
drizzle with 3 T olive oil & a sprinkle of salt.
Bake at 350°F (175°C) for 15 min.
(can be done several hours in advance)

15 min before serving, combine
toasted bread in a bowl with:

* 3 peaches, cubed
* 3 tomatoes, cubed
* 8 oz (225 g) fresh mozzarella, cubed
* 15 basil leaves, sliced

then toss all ingredients
with this vinaigrette
(can be made the day before):

⅓ c (75ml) olive oil
3 T red wine vinegar
1 clove garlic, minced
¼ t salt
¼ t pepper

Serve with more salt & pepper to taste

sesame FARRO salad

① COOK the FARRO

Boil a big pot of water & add 2 c (400 g) dry farro. Cook like pasta at a low boil for about 20 min, or until tender. Drain & rinse under cold water. (Can be cooked the day before.)

② TOSS COOLED FARRO WITH:

5 chopped scallions
2 c (40 g) arugula
2 T sunflower seeds

③ DRESS the SALAD

WHISK {
3 T olive oil
1 T soy sauce
3 T rice vinegar
1 T sesame oil
}

The dressing can be made ahead, but only dress the salad up to an hour before serving to keep the seeds crunchy & the greens from wilting.

④ ADD AVOCADO

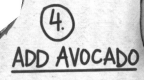

Sprinkle 1 large cubed avocado on top after dressing so it doesn't brown (avoid mixing it into the salad).

portobello & chimichurri

Lay 8 portobello mushrooms out on
a baking sheet (stems removed,
gills up) & drizzle with olive oil,
salt & pepper.

grill the mushrooms
on a hot BBQ for about 10 min
or roast in the oven
at 400°F (205°C) for 15-20 min

FOR THE CHIMICHURRI SAUCE:

1 bunch cilantro, stems included
1 bunch basil, stems included
4 scallions, roughly chopped
3 garlic cloves, peeled
¾ c (180 ml) olive oil
¼ c (60 ml) rice vinegar
½ t salt

blend well

serve 1 portobello per person, warm,
topped with about 2 T chimichurri

GRILLED PINEAPPLE

with cinnamon cream

(1) peel 2 pineapples &
slice into rounds
(can be cut the day before)

(2) grill on a
hot BBQ for
2 min per side

(or pan-fry in butter until golden)

(3) serve each person
1 or 2 rounds, warm or at
room temp, topped with
a dollop of cinnamon cream

FOR THE CINNAMON CREAM:
mix 2 c (480 ml)
whipped cream
with ½ t cinnamon

When we lived in New York City, we hosted a lot of theme parties. For some, we projected movies on our roof deck & guests dressed up as the characters from the film. In the woods we are a bit more low-key & on warm nights hang a sheet to project classic movies outdoors around the fire pit with friends.

brunch

menu serves 6-8

DO AHEAD: The day before, slice the grapefruit for the punch, defrost the puff pastry in the fridge overnight & make the coffee & chill. You can bake the Tomato Tart & the Zucchini Frittata Loaf at the same time a couple hours ahead & reheat.

SERVING SUGGESTIONS: Serve everything at once on a buffet (except the dessert). If you're low on time, serve juice or prosecco instead of the punch & just serve popsicles for dessert.

BUFFET SETUP

For easy buffet-style
serving, place stacks of
plates & napkins, glasses
& a jar or cup filled with
silverware at the end of
your food table or on a
side table. I love using
mismatched items. Set out
flowers & candles & use
a wooden box or stack of
wooden cutting boards to
add a bit of height.

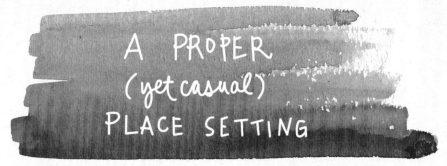

A PROPER (yet casual) PLACE SETTING

(because I can never remember which side the fork goes on!)

water glass →

wine glass →

salad fork

dinner fork

napkin

salad plate
—ON TOP OF—
dinner plate

knife

spoon

I often set up a buffet with stacks of mismatched plates, napkins & jars of silverware, but when I want to be "fancy," I set the table like this.

ruby
MIMOSA
punch

2 (750-ml) bottles prosecco, chilled
3 c (720 ml) ruby red grapefruit juice, chilled

mix in a small punch
bowl or large mixing
bowl right before serving

slice 2 grapefruits
into rounds & wedges
(can be done the day before)
(1 white & 1 ruby)

float the rounds on top of the punch
& lay out a plate of small
wedges cut to garnish each glass

cut

serve with a ladle

HEIRLOOM
Tomato Tart

makes two 8 by 8-in (20 by 20-cm) tarts
(8 generous servings)

lay out 2 sheets of defrosted puff pastry
(from a 17-oz/480-g box) on 2 baking sheets
(take the puff pastry out of the freezer
& put in the fridge the night before)

pinch the edges to
form a crust, then
spread ¾ c (180 ml)
ricotta on each sheet

(you'll need one 15-oz/425-g tub total)

sprinkle the ricotta layer
lightly with garlic powder &
salt, then bake for 15-20 min
at 375°F (190°C), or until golden

after baking, arrange 2-3
sliced tomatoes on each
crust, overlapping slightly

(you'll need 4-6 tomatoes total—look
for colorful heirloom ones)

Garnish each crust with ¼ c (10 g) freshly chopped cilantro &
2 t chopped chives, plus a sprinkle of olive oil, salt & pepper.
Slice each tart into quarters & serve at room temperature.

blueberry-pecan
SALAD

8 small handfuls arugula

1 c (120 g) chopped pecans

1 c (145 g) blueberries

4 oz (115 g) crumbled feta

lay arugula out on a large platter &
top with other ingredients

dress with your favorite vinaigrette

(or mine on page 16)

zucchini FRITTATA —loaf—

grate 4 zucchini over
a colander & press out
excess liquid

mix grated zucchini
in a big bowl with:

12 eggs

2 T fresh thyme

6 chopped scallions

1 t garlic powder

½ t salt

pour the mixture into a
9 by 5-inch (23 by 13-cm)
loaf pan lined with parchment
& bake for 1 hour at 375°F (190°C)
or until egg is set

use the parchment to lift the loaf out of the pan,
then slice and serve warm with salt & pepper

POPSICLE
affogato

1. make a 48-oz (1.5-L) pot of coffee the day before & chill overnight (decaf or regular)

2. using 8 store-bought chocolate popsicles, place each in an 6-oz (180-ml) cup of cold black coffee

Affogato is a traditional Italian dessert where a shot of espresso is poured over a scoop of ice cream. For this twist, I use chilled black coffee & store-bought Fudgsicles. Enjoy immediately, as it melts quickly!

picnic

menu serves 6-8

DO AHEAD: Make the lemonade & the orzo salad (except cilantro) the night before. For the feta salad, the onion and cucumber can be chopped the day before, and the rest of the vegetables can be cut several hours in advance. The wraps can be made several hours in advance. The cookies can be made the day before or baked a couple weeks in advance & frozen.

SERVING SUGGESTIONS: Set all items out on a blanket or buffet table for guests to serve themselves. If you're low on time, simply serve store-bought lemonade & cookies or fresh fruit for dessert (like berries or grapes).

GINGER-MINT
lemonade

1 c (50g) fresh mint leaves

¼ c (25g) chopped fresh ginger

64 oz (2L) lemonade

Mix all ingredients in a blender, then strain
(it's ok if some bits remain). Can be made the day before.
Pack in a large mason jar with lemon slices for a picnic
& serve over ice, if possible (or at least chilled). Shake or
stir before serving. Garnish with fresh lemon slices.

orzo-black bean salad

← —— 1½ c (170g) dry orzo

Cook the orzo in salted water according to package instructions (about 9 min), then drain & rinse under cold water. If making ahead, stir in 2 t olive oil to avoid sticking.

MIX COOKED ORZO WITH:

¼ red onion
(diced)

1 c (150 g) canned black beans
(drain & rinse)

1 red bell pepper
(seeded & cubed)

1 c (140 g) corn
(fresh or frozen)

¼ bunch cilantro, chopped
(leaves & stems)

DRESSING:

3 T olive oil, juice from 1 lime, ⅛ t salt, 1 t chili powder

This salad can be made a day ahead, but add cilantro & dressing no more than an hour before serving.

FETA CHOPPED SALAD

* 1 cucumber, cubed (I don't bother peeling)
* 2 large tomatoes, cubed
* ½ small red onion, cubed
* leaves from 2 sprigs mint, sliced
* ¾ c (115 g) crumbled feta (about 4 oz)

Toss all ingredients in a bowl with lemon juice, olive oil & salt

Vegetables can be chopped several hours in advance & refrigerated (onion & cucumber can be done the day before). Add feta & dressing just before packing for a picnic or before serving.

PESTO-CUCUMBER wraps

6 spinach tortillas

8 oz (225 g) cream cheese
(room temp)

2 cucumbers →
(cut into long spears—
no need to peel)

¾ c (180 ml)
store-bought
pesto

Spread cream cheese & pesto on each
tortilla, then add 3 long cucumber
spears & roll it up like a burrito. Wrap
a piece of parchment around the middle
& tie with twine. Can be made several
hours in advance.

3-ingredient brown sugar cookies

makes about 15 cookies

Cream together:

⅓ c (75 g) brown sugar

4 oz (115 g) salted butter (room temp)

then add in 1 c (125g) flour

mix well; it will be crumbly

press 2 T balls of dough together & place on baking sheet

OPTIONAL:
carefully press in pecans, pistachios, raisins, or dried cranberries

BAKE at 325°F (165°C) for 12-15 min, or until bottoms are golden.

Lunch Gathering

menu serves 6-8

DO AHEAD: Make the berry-thyme ice cubes the day before. Slice the cucumber for the Cucumber Caprese Bites. All the toppings for the Arugula Niçoise Salad can be prepared the night before & stored in the fridge. The quinoa can be cooked the night before.

SERVING SUGGESTIONS: Serve the punch & Cucumber Caprese Bites to start as guests arrive. Set the 2 salads & dressing on the dining table or on a buffet for guests to serve themselves. I like to also put out a nice rustic loaf of bread with butter on the side. Serve fruit, chocolates, or store-bought cookies for dessert, or ask a guest to bring something. If you're low on time, serve juice & seltzer instead of the punch & a wedge of cheese with crackers as an appetizer instead of the Cucumber Caprese Bites.

berry-thyme punch

① Freeze

make berry-thyme ice cubes by placing
3 raspberries, 1 sprig thyme & water to cover
into cupcake tins & freezing overnight

(6 oz /170g raspberries makes about 12 cubes)

② Muddle

{ 10 sprigs thyme
{ 10 hulled strawberries

Mash these in a mixing bowl or small punch bowl
using the bottom of a glass. Use a fork to remove
stems & large berry pieces, leaving some pulp.

③ Mix

Stir in 5 c (1.2L) chilled
cran-raspberry juice, 8 oz
(240 ml) vodka (if you wish) &
8 sliced strawberries. Right
before serving add 4 c (960 ml)
chilled seltzer.

float a few berry-thyme
ice cubes in the bowl &
serve with a ladle

colorful
paper
straws
are a fun
addition

a mixing bowl
works well as
a small-batch
punch bowl

*can also
be made
in a
Pitcher

Set out
dishes of extra
ice cubes & thyme
sprigs for garnish

(ice cubes fit in wide-mouth glasses)

123

cucumber caprese bites

on a toothpick, stack:

1 cherry tomato,
then 1 basil leaf,
then 1 cucumber square,
then 1 mozzarella ball

For 8 servings (24 bites), you'll need about
1 pint (290 g) cherry tomatoes, 1 bunch of basil,
2 cucumbers & 16 oz (455 g) mini mozzarella balls.
The cucumbers can be sliced the day before.

drizzle with olive oil & salt before serving

Arugula Niçoise Salad

8 small handfuls arugula

16 oz (455 g) mini potatoes,
roasted with olive oil & salt
at 425°F (220°C) for 25-30 min,
or until tender

8 oz (225 g) baked marinated tofu
(I buy prebaked teriyaki flavor)

1 c (145 g) cherry tomatoes, halved

6 hard-boiled eggs, peeled & halved

8 oz (225 g) sliced fresh
green beans, ends trimmed

½ c (75 g) pitted Kalamata olives

Lay out arugula on a
large platter & top with
"stripes" of all other ingredients

sprinkle 2 T capers over the whole platter

DRESS WITH YOUR FAVORITE VINAIGRETTE OR MINE ON PAGE 16

* all toppings can be prepped the day before

Quinoa Crunch Salad

cook 1½ c (255 g) dry red quinoa
according to package instructions
(can be cooked the day before)

Mix cooked quinoa with a handful each of:

sunflower seeds
pistachios
pecans, chopped
almonds, sliced
pumpkin seeds
dried cherries

dress with olive oil, lemon juice & salt

the quinoa can be made
the day before, but mix
in the nuts right before
serving to keep them crunchy

Fall Feast

menu serves 6-8

DO AHEAD: The pomegranate ice ring needs to be made the day before. Bake the butternut squash for the crostini & the acorn squash for the lasagna at the same time, up to a day before. The baguette can be toasted for the crostini a couple hours in advance. Pears can be sliced ahead, but brush with lemon to avoid browning. You can assemble the lasagna while the carrots are cooking a few hours ahead. Put the lasagna in the oven an hour before you plan to eat.

SERVING SUGGESTIONS: Serve the drink & crostini as guests arrive & set all other items out on a buffet. The galette is meant for dessert & can be baked that morning or during dinner.

at the pumpkin patch
in nearby Half Moon Bay, CA

pomegranate PUNCH

Make an ice ring by pouring seeds from
1 pomegranate & water (to the top)
into a Bundt pan. Freeze overnight.

2 (750-ml)
bottles prosecco,
chilled

1 (750-ml)
bottle sparkling
apple-pomegranate cider

(or just sparkling apple cider)

Mix prosecco & sparkling cider
in a small punch bowl or large
mixing bowl. Add the ice ring
just as guests arrive, as it may
melt quickly. Serve with a ladle
& extra pomegranate seeds
for garnish.

butternut & goat cheese crostini

toast slices from 1 baguette:
cut ½-in (12-mm) slices & drizzle
with olive oil & salt, then broil
on one side for about 2 min on high
(can be done a few hours ahead)

1 small butternut squash:
peel & cut into ¼-in (6-mm) cubes, then roast
at 400°F (205°C) with olive oil, salt & pepper
for 20-25 min, or until golden, turning a
couple of times (can be done the day before)

spread goat cheese on crostini:
put 1-2 t chevre on each toasted slice

sprinkle all the crostini with:
roasted butternut cubes, fresh thyme
leaves, flaky salt & olive oil

Kale-Hazelnut Salad

2 pears, thinly sliced

(slice just before serving or, if done ahead, brush with lemon to prevent browning)

¾ c (100g) hazelnuts, chopped

8 small handfuls baby kale

(you can also use mixed greens or arugula)

seeds from 1 pomegranate

4 oz (115g) shaved hard pecorino (1 use a peeler)

Up to an hour before serving, place kale in a big bowl & toss with your favorite vinaigrette or mine on page 16. Scatter all other ingredients on top of the greens so they are visible, mixing just a bit in. Drizzle a little more dressing over the top. It's also beautiful served on a large platter.

zaatar roasted carrots

Zaatar
(a Middle Eastern spice mix)

①

trim the tops off
2 lbs (910g) med carrots,
leaving just a bit

(2-3 carrots per person)

②.

Lay carrots out on a baking sheet & drizzle
generously with olive oil (about 3 T) & 1 T zaatar.
Roll carrots with your fingers to coat well.
Sprinkle with salt, pepper & red pepper flakes,
then bake at 400°F (205°C) for 20 min, or until tender.
(can be roasted a few hours ahead)

③.

Serve whole carrots on a platter garnished
with Greek yogurt, cilantro & sesame seeds

(warm or at room temp)

SQUASH LASAGNA

start with 1 large
(2-3 lb / 1-1.5 Kg) acorn squash
(or 2 small ones)

Cut in half, remove seeds & bake
for 1 hour at 400°F (205°C) or until
a knife goes in easily. Scoop out
the flesh & mash with a fork.
(can be done the day before).

YOU'LL NEED

5 c (1.2 L) marinara sauce
9 no-boil lasagna noodles
16 oz (455g) ricotta
mashed squash (see above)
3 chopped scallions
¼ c (9g) chopped sage
3 c (330g) grated mozzarella
salt, pepper & garlic powder

Spread some sauce in the bottom of a 9 by 13-in (23 by 33-cm) baking
dish, then layer each ingredient (roughly) in the order written
above, repeating 3 times, sprinkling salt, pepper & garlic powder
every couple layers. You can also use fresh minced garlic. Save
some of the mozzarella to sprinkle on top. This can be assembled or
made several hours ahead & baked or reheated before serving.

Bake at 375°F (190°C) for 45 min

Pear-Thyme galettes

*makes 2

YOU'LL NEED:

* 2 (8 by 8-in/20 by 20-cm) puff pastry sheets (from a 17-oz/480-g box)
* ¼ c (60 ml) fig jam
* 2-3 pears, thinly sliced (no need to peel)
* 3 T chopped raw walnuts
* 2 T crumbled Gorgonzola cheese
* 2 t fresh thyme leaves
* 2 t melted butter mixed with 2 t honey

Lay the puff pastry sheets out on 2 baking sheets & snip off the corners (discard corner dough). Spread a thin layer of fig jam over each, leaving a small border. Lay the pears out in a circular pattern over the jam, overlapping a bit. Sprinkle walnuts, Gorgonzola, thyme & the honey-butter mixture over the pears. Fold the edges of the dough to form a round tart.

BAKE at 400°F (205°c) for 20 min

Allow to cool & use a spoon to remove any excess juices. Makes 2 (8-inch/20-cm) galettes, which is 8 generous servings or 12 smaller ones. If you have just 6 guests, you can halve the recipe; 1 galette sliced & served with vanilla ice cream should be plenty. If you don't love strong blue cheese, you may consider omitting the Gorgonzola. This can be made ahead & served at room temp, or prepared ahead & baked during dinner.

picking flowers for
the table with Ezra
in the garden

A cluster of seasonal produce,
candles & mini bouquets makes a simple
centerpiece that's easy to see over.
For this fall table I chose items that
were yellow, orange, red & magenta.

cocktail party

menu serves 8-10

DO AHEAD: Slice the lemons for the drinks, prepare & refrigerate the fillings for the Endive Bar & slice the cucumbers. Toast the bread for the crostini a few hours ahead. Prepare the avocado mixture for the crostini a few hours before & store in an airtight container. The Spicy Chocolate Almonds can be made several days before.

SERVING SUGGESTIONS: Serve everything at once on a buffet table. If you're low on time, just make one cocktail, skip the Truffled Cucumber Rounds & simply serve chocolate for dessert.

SETTING UP THE BAR

We like to pull our antique bar cart outdoors for parties to let guests mix their own cocktails. We stock it with whiskey, vodka, gin & seltzer, plus a cocktail shaker, mixing glass, bar spoon, jigger, ice bucket, straws & bitters. I also have a few vintage seltzer bottles that I like to put out for decoration. We set up a separate bar area with wine, beer, juice & nonalcoholic options, as well as garnishes like slices of lemon or lime.

use watercolors
to paint stripes
& splatters on
shipping tags to
label pitchers
& decanters
for the bar

VODKA

RUM

BOURBON

GIN

seltzer

Rosé Spritzer

COMBINE IN A PITCHER

- 2 (750-ml) bottles Rosé wine
- 1 (750-ml) bottle seltzer
- about 15 drops Angostura bitters
- 1 lemon, thinly sliced in rounds

serve in wine glasses
over ice with a lemon slice
(lemons can be sliced the day before)

KUMQUAT GIMLET PUNCH

MIX IN A PITCHER:

- juice from 6 limes
- ½ c (100 g) sugar
- 4 c (945 ml) water

STIR

Stir until sugar
dissolves, then add 24 oz
(750 ml) gin, plus a few lime
slices, kumquat slices & whole
kumquats. Serve over
glasses of ice.

GARNISH

Garnish glasses with lime
slices & kumquat swizzle sticks.
Prep the swizzle sticks by placing
3 kumquats onto a small wooden
skewer to put inside each glass.
(Can be made the day before.)

• If kumquats are out of season,
use orange or mandarin slices in the punch &
green grapes for the swizzle sticks.

endive bar

5-7 endives, leaves separated

Pomegranate seeds

salted sunflower seeds

butternut squash

roast ¼-inch (6-mm) cubes at 400°F (205°C) with olive oil & salt for 25 min, or until soft & golden, turning a couple of times

crumbled Gorgonzola cheese

ricotta or cream cheese

red onion

chop 1 med onion & caramelize in a pan with 1 T butter, 1 T olive oil & a pinch of salt

chopped scallions

seedless red grapes, halved

fresh thyme leaves

On a platter, lay out small bowls of each ingre_____
guests to build their own endive cups with desire_____
a base of cheese & piling 2 or 3 toppings over it. Other filling ideas incl_____
pine nuts, cherry tomatoes & feta. All toppings can be prepped the night before.

butternut, caramelized onions & Gorgonzola

caramelized onions, scallions & sunflower seeds

ricotta, scallions & sunflower seeds

cream cheese, scallions & grapes

Gorgonzola, grapes & sunflower seeds

ricotta, thyme, pomegranate & butternut

FLAVOR combination IDEAS

avocado-tahini crostini

① BROIL

Diagonally slice a baguette into ¼-in (6-mm) slices, drizzle with olive oil & salt, and broil on high for 2 min, or until golden on top.

(can be done 2-3 hours ahead & stored in a sealed bag)

② MASH

3 ripe avocados
3 T tahini paste
1½ t garlic powder
salt & pepper

→ spread about 2 t of the avocado mixture on each crostini

③ SPRINKLE the crostini with flaky salt & red pepper flakes

The avocado mixture can be made up to 2 hours ahead, but keep it airtight in the fridge & stir before using. Spread it on the crostini just before serving as it may start to turn brown after about an hour. This makes about 30 crostini.

TRUFFLED CUCUMBER ROUNDS

← slice 2 cucumbers into ½-in (12-mm) rounds

← top each round with a 1 t dollop of ricotta

(You'll need about ¾ c/185 g ricotta total. I spoon it into a plastic bag, snip the corner off & pipe the ricotta on.)

sprinkle truffle salt, sunflower seeds, & chopped chives over the ricotta

(You'll need about ¼ c/70 g sunflower seeds & ½ bunch chives total.)

spicy chocolate almonds

melt 6 oz (170 g) semisweet chocolate chips over a double boiler

(I use a glass bowl over a pot of boiling water)

stir in 1½ c (210 g) roasted, unsalted almonds until well coated

RAW SUGAR

Use a spoon to make small mounds (about 8 almonds each) on a sheet of parchment paper. Sprinkle lightly with coarse raw sugar, coarse or flaky salt & cayenne pepper. Allow to harden (about 1 hour at room temperature, or 15 min in the refrigerator). Store in a cool, airtight place. Can be made several days in advance.

CAYENNE PEPPER

I USE FLAKY MALDON SALT

OUR COCKTAIL PARTY SETUP

bar

food table ↑

standing room near the bar

sitting area using indoor chairs

In addition to a special cocktail, we usually put out water, wine, beer & a couple nonalcoholic options.

165

vegan & gluten-free gathering

menu serves 6-8

DO AHEAD: The night before, slice the cucumbers & limes for the drinks, make the hummus, slice the bell peppers & prepare the ingredients for the tacos (except the mint).

SERVING SUGGESTIONS: Serve the coolers & hummus as guests arrive & set all other items on a buffet. For dessert, try serving fresh fruit kebabs or the Strawberry-Balsamic Sundaes on page 34 with a nondairy ice cream.

DIY EMAIL INVITATION

come on over!

BRUNCH
Sunday at 11am

dinner
PARTY
SAT. JUNE 8th, 7pm

GRILLED
CHEESE
PARTY!!!

COCKTAIL
PARTY
this Saturday! 6pm

LET'S
celebrate!
DRINKS AT OUR PLACE
SAT. SEPTEMBER 1, 5pm

DINNER
PARTY!
Sat. May 12, 8PM

RYAN'S
BDAY
PARTY!

For occasions when sending a paper invitation seems like too much, I still like to tell guests about the event in a personal way. Try adding a custom photo to an email, instead of using an online invitation service. I write with a black marker on a piece of paper, scatter pretty items around it & take a picture with my phone to paste into an email with more written information. For best results, shoot midday outdoors in the shade without flash, with your camera directly above the invitation. Try arranging colorful items like flowers, leaves, produce, silverware, a cutting board, napkins, plates, glasses, candles, ribbons, or photos around the paper. Choose 1 or 2 colors to repeat (like my yellow & green color scheme at right). ⟶

DINNER
PARTY!
Sat. May 12, 8PM

Cucumber-Lime COOLERS

mix in a pitcher:

* **64 oz (2 L) limeade** (or lemonade)
* **8 oz (240 ml) seltzer**
* **slices from 1 lime**
* **ice**

VODKA

← optional: add 8 oz (240 ml) vodka to the pitcher or 1 shot to each drink

Prepare glasses with long, thin cucumber spears & lime slices for garnish (both can be sliced ahead). One cucumber should be enough for 8 drinks.

Butternut Hummus

← — Roast half a squash:

Slice a med butternut squash in half lengthwise & remove seeds. Lay 1 half of the squash face down on an oiled baking sheet & roast at 425°F (220°C) for 30-40 min, or until fork-tender. Cool a bit then scoop the flesh out into a food processor. (Can be done ahead.)

Blend roasted squash with:

- 1 (15-oz/425-g) can of chickpeas, drained
- ¼ c (60 ml) olive oil
- 1 t paprika
- ¼ t salt
- 1 t garlic powder (or 3 cloves, minced)
- juice from 1 lemon

Spoon into a bowl & sprinkle the top with paprika, olive oil & coarse salt.

Serve with slices of red, yellow, or orange bell peppers

* can be made up to 2 days in advance & kept in the refrigerator

Vietnamese Lentil Tacos

2 grated
CARROTS

5 chopped
SCALLIONS

leaves from 5
sprigs fresh
MINT

3 thinly sliced mini
CUCUMBERS
(or 1 regular)

**CORN
TORTILLAS**
(2-3 per person)

3 (15-oz/425-g) cans
cooked black
LENTILS

1 bunch thinly sliced
RADISHES

TOPPINGS

nondairy sour cream
3 mashed avocados
Sriracha
lime wedges
coarse salt

Drain the lentils & heat in a pan for 3-5 min with a pinch of salt, pepper, garlic powder & Sriracha. (I use black lentils, but you can use any kind, dry or canned.) Wrap tortillas in foil & warm in the oven (separate into packs of about 6). Carrots, scallions, cucumbers, radishes & limes can all be prepared in advance & stored in the fridge. Serve items in bowls so guests can make their own tacos on a buffet.

Roasted Eggplant Salad

① CUBE
→ 1 big eggplant
↘ 2 med onions

② ROAST with olive oil, salt & pepper for 40 min at 425°F (220°C)

③ TOSS cooled eggplant & onion with 4 cubed small cucumbers & 4 cubed tomatoes

drizzle with more olive oil
& coarse salt before serving

optional: garnish with edible flowers – see pages 22 & 24

Use small cups like these Moroccan tea glasses to make small bouquets that are easy to see over the table

Mix store-bought flowers with foraged greenery in mason jars for a more natural & whimsical look

place votive candles in small jars on plates around the room or on the table

winter Feast

menu serves 6-8

DO AHEAD: The chowder can be made up to 2 days in advance. The clementine ice ring must be made the day before. Slice the clementines for the cocktail & cook the onions & leeks for the Caramelized Onion Bake the day before. You can bake the Caramelized Onion Bake a few hurs before & reheat before serving. The garlic can be baked the day before.

SERVING SUGGESTIONS: Serve the cocktails & Baked Garlic with Brie as guests arrive & the other dishes on a buffet. The chowder can be kept warm in a slow-cooker on a buffet table, or have a guest help you dish up & pass out bowls for each person. If you're low on time, skip the cocktail & the brie & just serve wine & cheese to start.

CITRUS AS DÉCOR

*trim both ends &
an orange becomes a vase!*
(tip: carnations do well out of water for hours)

*lemon
napkin
weight*

*use clementines to display
buffet signs or place cards*

clementine
cocktails

SWEET
POTATO
CHOWDER

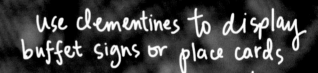

Paint stripes on an unlined
index card, fold in half, write
with a marker, then tape onto a
short kebab stick. Push it into a
clementine or an inverted lemon,
lime, or orange half.

DIY PLACE SETTING

At each place setting, write your guest's name on a painted shipping tag (see page 151) & tie it around a napkin. Tuck in a little flower or leaf & place the napkin on the plate with a clementine or any seasonal piece of fruit.

Write a question on the back of each tag & go around the table so each guest can answer aloud. It's a fun way to get the conversation started. Some ideas: What's the best thing that's happened to you this month? What's the most delicious thing you've eaten recently? Who is your dream lunch date? What's the best trip you've taken? If you could go anywhere on your next vacation, where would it be? If you could switch careers, what would you choose? What's the best (or worst) movie you've seen this year?

CLEMENTINE COCKTAILS

for the ICE RING:
freeze 4 sliced clementines in a Bundt pan with water overnight

slice extra clementines for garnish at the same time & refrigerate until serving

COMBINE

4 c (960 ml) clementine juice (or orange juice)

4 c (960 ml) seltzer

8 oz (240 ml) bourbon

Angostura bitters (about 15 drops)

Mix all ingredients in a small punch bowl or large mixing bowl & serve with a ladle. Add the ice ring just as guests arrive. Let guests make their own sugar rimmed glasses by rubbing the glass edge with a half clementine, then dipping it in a small dish of raw sugar. Garnish with a straw pushed through the center of a round clementine slice. Use mandarins if you can't find clementines.

BAKED GARLIC
with Brie

Cut the tops off 3-5 heads of garlic & peel off excess skin. Place in foil & drizzle with olive oil. Close foil & bake at 400°F (205°C) for 45 min, or until garlic cloves are soft (can be baked the day before).

slice a baguette diagonally

drizzle with olive oil & salt, then broil on a baking sheet until golden (about 2 min)

serve the baked garlic & toasted baguette with a large wedge of triple-cream Brie

Serve the garlic warm or at room temp. Let guests top their own baguette slices with garlic, Brie & flaky salt. A fork works well to remove & mash the garlic cloves.

sweet potato chowder

serves 8-10

SAUTÉ IN A BIG POT FOR 5 MIN:

* 1 large onion, diced
* 1 T curry powder
* 3 cloves garlic, minced
* 2 T olive oil
* pinch each salt & pepper

THEN ADD:

* 6 sweet potatoes, unpeeled & cubed
* 2 c (480 ml) unsweetened coconut milk
* 4 c (960 ml) vegetable broth

Simmer on med/low for about 25 min or until the potatoes are tender. Use a hand blender to carefully puree the whole pot while hot. Add a little more broth or coconut milk if it seems too thick. The soup can be made a day or 2 ahead & reheated.

Garnish with Greek yogurt, pomegranate seeds & chopped scallions

CRISPY KALE
with paprika & truffle salt

①
chop 2 bunches kale
into 1-in (2.5-cm) pieces
(remove thick stem ends)

②
Spread kale out
on 2 baking sheets
& sprinkle with:

- 2 T OLIVE OIL
- 1 t SMOKED PARIKA
- ¼ t TRUFFLE SALT

The less the pieces overlap, the
crunchier they will be. But I like
the contrast of having some pieces
softer, so I let them overlap a bit.

③
Roast at 425°F (220°C)
for 5-8 min, or until bright green
with charred tips (watch closely).

* best cooked right before serving, if possible, to maintain crispness

caramelized onion bake

2 leeks
3 onions

Slice the leeks (just the white part) & onions thinly & sauté in a big skillet with olive oil & butter for 40 min, covered, stirring every several min. The pan will seem very full at first, but they reduce a lot. Keep the heat on med/low for the first half, then switch to low. This can be done the day before.

Mix the cooled caramelized onion mixture in a bowl with:

1 c (100g) grated Parmesan
6 large eggs
¼ c (60ml) milk (any %)

plus a pinch each salt & pepper

Pour the mixture into a greased 9 by 13-inch (23 by 33-cm) baking dish & sprinkle 3 chopped scallions on top.

Bake at 350°F (175°C) for 25–30 min, then remove from the oven & place the dough of 8 large store-bought biscuits on top. Sprinkle with Parmesan, salt, pepper & olive oil, then bake for another 15 min, or until the onion mixture is set & the biscuits are golden. This can be prepared ahead, refrigerated & baked before serving, or baked a few hours ahead & reheated.

cider floats

sparkling apple cider

ginger beer

hand cider

(you'll need 1-2 bottles of each)

1 apple, diced

1 c (240 ml) whipped cream

½ c (120 ml) caramel sauce

2 pints (946 ml) vanilla ice cream

Put 1-2 scoops vanilla ice cream in a cup & pour in cider or ginger beer. Top with whipped cream, caramel sauce, diced apple & a pinch of nutmeg & serve with a spoon. It's fun to bring all the ingredients to the table after dinner & let guests build their own floats.

centerpiece on a platter

Create an easy centerpiece for your
table by arranging candles & fresh,
seasonal produce on a platter or tray.
Then cut short flower stems & push them
into the gaps. Look for flowers that
do well out of water, like carnations &
mums. Use pillar candles in different
heights or votives in jars.

holiday cocktail party

DO AHEAD: Mix the cider, make the Pastry-Wrapped Olives & caramelize the onions for the Polenta Pizzas the night before. The olives and pizzas can be baked at the same time. The fudge can be made up to 2 days before or up to a few weeks in advance & frozen.

SERVING SUGGESTIONS: Serve all items at the same time on a buffet table. If you're low on time, just make 1 cocktail, skip the Pastry-Wrapped Olives & serve chocolate truffles for dessert.

Floral Garland

Using a needle & sturdy thread
(I use pastry twine), string short
stemmed flowers, fresh cranberries
& leaves to make a garland,
placing items a few inches apart.
These are beautiful hung above a
bar or table or in a doorway. Make
a long garland to hang beside
twinkle lights over a patio. Poms,
carnations & mums work well for
this as they won't wilt out of
water. Other fun items to string
include fresh kumquats & okra.

tie the ends to nails
or tacks, or use washi
tape to secure it to a wall

RUM-PEAR
cider

64 oz
(2L)
pear
juice

8 oz
(240 ml)
dark
rum

1
pinch
nutmeg

3
cinnamon
sticks

1
apple
+ 2 t
cloves

Combine the juice, rum, nutmeg & cinnamon sticks in a slow-cooker. Use a toothpick to make holes in an apple & push cloves in all around. Add the clove apple to the slow-cooker & heat on high for 1 hour, or until hot. Serve in mugs garnished with additional cinnamon sticks & star anise.

I use a tea towel to dress up my slow-cooker

Bubbly Cran-Rosemary

2 (750-ml) bottles prosecco, chilled →

3 c (720 ml) white cranberry juice
(or white grape juice)

20 drops Angostura bitters

Mix all ingredients in a pitcher or punch bowl with ice, fresh cranberries & a few sprigs of rosemary. Prepare glasses ahead of time with a few fresh cranberries & a sprig of rosemary as garnish & let guests serve themselves.

CHEESE BOARD SPREAD

1-2 oz
(30-55g)
cheese
per person
total

I like using
basil leaves as
"crackers" to eat
creamy cheese on

- fresh baguette
- rice crackers
- wheat crackers

{ goat Gouda
triple-cream Brie
sheep Manchego

(or choose 1 goat, 1 cow & 1 sheep,
ranging from hard to creamy)

dried pears & figs

fig jam

honey

red
grapes

apple & pear
slices

olives

(if you're making the
Pastry-Wrapped Olives
on page 210, choose
different olives
here, or skip)

Marcona
almonds

macadamia
nuts

cornichons

(salted)

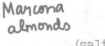

For a warm-weather cheese board, try using
fresh peaches, strawberry jam, cherry tomatoes & melon.

polenta pizzas

① Caramelize 2 red onions:

Thinly slice the onions & cook in a pan
with 3 T olive oil & a pinch of salt on
med/low. Keep covered and stir occasionally
for about 25 min, or until very soft &
golden. Then chop & stir in ⅓ c (35 g)
marinated sun-dried tomatoes.

POLENTA

SUN-DRIED TOMATOES

② Top polenta with marinara, onions & walnuts:

Slice 2 (18-oz/510-g) tubes of precooked
polenta into rounds. Lay polenta out on
an oiled baking sheet & top each with
1 t marinara (you'll need about ½ c/
120 ml total), 1 T caramelized onion
mixture & about 1 t chopped walnuts
(you'll need about ½ c/60 g total).

optional: add cheese!

MARINARA

WALNUTS

③ Bake at 375°F (190°C) for 15 min, or until hot.

• •

The onions can be caramelized the day before. The pizzas can be assembled
a couple hours in advance & heated before serving. This recipe makes about
24 mini pizzas. They are ideal hot but are also good at room temperature.

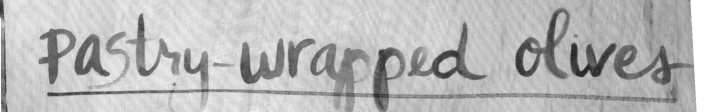

Pastry-wrapped olives

use a paper towel to dry off
about 25 pitted, stuffed olives

I prefer olives stuffed with
pimentos, garlic, or blue cheese

use jar lids or a small glass
(approx 2 in/5 cm) to cut circles
from 2 sheets of 8 by 8-in
(20 by 20-cm) puff pastry

wrap each olive entirely in the puff
pastry, snip off excess dough, roll
in your hands & place on a greased
baking sheet, pinched side down

pinch
closed

sprinkle each with grated Parmesan

BAKE at 375°F (190°C)
for 20 min, or until golden

These can be made the day before & served warm or at room temp.
Serve with mustard or your favorite dipping sauce.

SALTED FUDGE
with cinnamon

BOIL & STIR FOR 3 MIN

3 c (600 g) sugar
1½ c (340 g) butter
⅔ c (165 ml) evaporated milk

THEN ADD

12 oz (340 g) semisweet chocolate chips
7 oz (200 g) marshmallow creme
½ t cinnamon

↓

stir over low heat until well combined

I use Maldon salt ↘

Line a 9 by 13-in (23 by 33-cm) pan with parchment & pour in chocolate mixture. Sprinkle with flaky salt & allow to cool in the freezer until hard (about 15 min). Using the parchment, pull the whole fudge block out of the pan & onto a cutting board & use a large chef's knife to slice. Makes about 48 bite-size squares. Can be made a few days before or up to a few weeks ahead & frozen. Send extras home with guests (see page 214) or freeze

Hostess Gift Ideas

Package a few squares of fudge into a plastic bag tied with pastry twine & a sprig of greenery. It makes a sweet gift for guests to take home after a holiday party or to give as a hostess gift (recipe page 212). Some of my other favorite hostess gifts include beeswax votive candles, a bouquet of fresh herbs in a jar, or a nice bottle of olive oil.

mantel decorated with fresh greens, persimmons & limes

weeknight gathering

menu serves 6-8

SERVING SUGGESTIONS: If you're having people over on a weeknight, this is an easy menu you can put together after work. The shishitos can be an appetizer or served with the meal. If you're low on time, skip the shishitos & serve nuts or cheese to start. I serve everything at once, passing bowls around the table family-style. Serving Champagne will make any weeknight feel like a special occasion! Sliced French bread & butter are a great side with this meal. For dessert, serve store-bought cookies or chocolates, or make simple sundaes by topping vanilla ice cream with a dollop of peanut butter & a drizzle of honey.

Blistered Shishitos

16 oz (455g) whole shishito peppers

(if you can't find shishitos, you can use mini sweet peppers)

Lay the peppers out on a baking sheet & coat well with a generous amount of olive oil (about 2 T). Sprinkle with coarse or flaky salt (like Maldon).

Roast at 425°F (220°C) about 10 min, or until browned

Shishitos are so delicious, but enjoy with caution! About 1 in 10 of these little peppers is spicy (I don't do super spicy, but I can handle these). The seeds tend to be the spiciest part. Serve alongside a little dish to discard stems & seeds.

CRUNCHY
green salad

8 small handfuls greens
(mixed greens, baby kale, or arugula)

½ c (65g) pepitas
(shelled pumpkin seeds)

½ c (75g)
golden raisins

2 apples,
cubed

1 English cucumber, cubed

Serve about 1 handful of greens per person. Combine all
ingredients in a bowl or on a large platter & serve with your
favorite vinaigrette (or mine on page 16). Cucumbers & apples can be
sliced ahead. Brush the apple slices with lemon to prevent browning.

zucchini + herbs

Slice 6 zucchini into sticks:
(can be done ahead)

1 **2** **3**

Sauté zucchini in a skillet over med heat
with 2 T olive oil, ⅛ t garlic powder (or
2 cloves garlic, minced) & ⅛ t salt until
slightly browned & tender, about 7 min. Best
served warm within an hour of cooking.

Parsley
& basil
also work!

Just before serving, sprinkle
with fresh cilantro
& grated parmesan

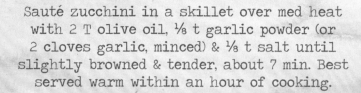

pesto gnocchi

2 (17-oz/500-g) packages gnocchi

Follow package instructions, or boil
gnocchi until they float (about 3 min),
then drain. These are best made just before
serving. I usually boil the water as
guests arrive & toss the gnocchi in right
before we sit down at the table.

toss cooked gnocchi with about ½ c (120 ml)
store-bought pesto & spread out on a platter

sprinkle about 2 T sunflower
seeds & 2 T grated Parmesan
over the gnocchi

serve hot

PARTY BUFFETS
bar-style serving

Bar-style buffets are great for hosting small or large groups & can often more easily accommodate guests with food restrictions. Many of the items on these menus can be prepared in advance & served at room temperature. You don't need to serve all the items I list on each menu; please use my suggestions as a starting point & be creative with your own additions.

BREAKFAST TACO BAR

corn tortillas

I like to heat tortillas over an open flame on the stove. But to warm several at once, wrap packs of 6 tortillas in foil & put them in the oven at 350°F (175°C) for about 15 min.

scrambled eggs

about 2 per person

cubed sweet potatoes

sauté with olive oil, garlic, salt & pepper

grated Jack cheese

refried beans

black beans

This is a great way to host a brunch for a large group, since most of the items can be prepared ahead & set out at room temperature. You can prepare everything the night before except the eggs, cilantro & avocado. Warm the tortillas, eggs, potatoes & beans before serving & keep covered to stay warm. The quinoa & cauliflower can be served warm or at room temp. Keep the tortillas in foil or a towel.

quinoa

stir in chili powder,
garlic powder, olive
oil, salt & pepper

cauliflower

chop & roast for 20 min
at 425°F (220°C) with olive
oil, paprika & salt

avocado

slice or mash
into guacamole &
sprinkle with
lemon or lime juice
to prevent browning

diced
red
onion

chopped
scallions

thinly
sliced
radishes

pomegranate
seeds

cilantro

salsa
& lime
wedges

CAULIFLOWER

BLACK
BEANS

REFRIED
BEANS

QUINOA

Make simple buffet signs
by painting a patch of watercolor
on a folded index card & writing with a black pen

RICE NOODLE BAR

I use maifun rice sticks & follow package cooking instructions. They are easy to prepare & usually just require a 10-min soak in boiling hot water. This type of rice noodle does well when cooled & doesn't stick together, but it's a good idea to toss with oil after draining to keep noodles separated.

rice noodles ⟶

marinated tofu

eggplant
cube & sauté with olive oil, garlic & salt

avocado
slice before serving & sprinkle with lemon or lime juice to avoid browning

cubed cucumber
no need to peel

chickpeas
I use canned, drain them & toss with olive oil, salt & pepper

edamame
buy them shelled

All ingredients can be prepared ahead (except for the herbs & avocado) & served at room temp. The polenta is best fried up to an hour before serving. You don't need to serve all of these toppings—feel free to add some of your own! Sauce is key & be sure to serve olive oil, sesame oil, soy sauce & rice vinegar on the side as dressings.

fresh herbs
basil, mint, cilantro

purple cabbage

bean sprouts

Scallions

hot sauce, peanuts & lime

crispy polenta
cube a precooked tube of polenta & fry in olive oil

corn

peanut sauce

→ store-bought or make your own

3 T peanut butter
1 T sesame oil
3 T olive oil
1 T soy sauce

make a handwritten list of toppings on paper or a chalkboard

RICE NOODLE BAR

.... TOPPINGS ....

CHICK-PEAS
CRISPY POLENTA
BASIL
CILANTRO
MINT
LIME
CORN
CABBAGE
EDAMAME

SRIRACHA
PEANUT SAUCE
PEANUTS
BEAN SPROUTS
SCALLIONS
AVOCADO
TOFU
CUCUMBER
EGGPLANT

GRILLED CHEESE PARTY

We host an annual grilled cheese party on my birthday because it's my favorite
thing to eat! We put a bar of all the fixings on the picnic table & let guests build
their dream sandwiches. Then we put our biggest skillet on the BBQ & grill the sandwiches
on the deck with everyone. That way, no one is stuck in the kitchen. It also works well
to plug in a few electric skillets or panini presses outside & let guests cook their own
sandwiches. If you're making them on the stove, use a covered skillet, butter the bread
first & cook the sandwiches on med/low for about 3 minutes on each side. You don't need to
serve all the items below. Use this list as a starting point & be creative! A slow-cooker
full of soup (like my Sweet Potato Chowder on page 188) works well on the side.

breads & spreads

baguette

ciabatta   sourdough   olive   wheat

mayo   mustard   pesto   harissa   fig jam
                                        red pepper spread

cheeses & fillings

Brie
St. André
& regular

gruyère

Sharp
Cheddar

gouda

mozzarella

tomatoes

colorful heirloom if possible

dill
pickles

avocado

sprinkle with
lemon or lime juice
to prevent browning

arugula

basil

chives

sage

caramelized onions

thinly slice & sauté onions in
a big skillet with butter, olive
oil & salt on med/low for about
30 min, or until golden

balsamic pears

thinly slice pears (skin on) & sauté in
a pan on med/low with butter, balsamic
vinegar & a pinch of salt for 5-10 min,
or until slightly softened

237

MAYO

MUSTARD

HARISSA

PESTO

MOZZARELLA

SHARP CHEDDAR

GOUDA

GRUYÈRE

BRIE

SAINT ANDRÉ

BASIL

SAGE

CHIVES

Cover a table with brown postal or wrapping paper & label items with a black marker. Decorate the table with fresh produce & herbs. Lay collard greens under plates & cutting boards & place artichokes, radishes, thyme & citrus around the edges.

favorite combinations:
* sourdough | harissa | Cheddar | chives
* baguette | fig jam | Saint André | arugula
* wheat | Gouda | apple | basil
* olive bread | Gruyère | caramelized onions
* ciabatta | brie | sage
* sourdough | Gouda | balsamic pears

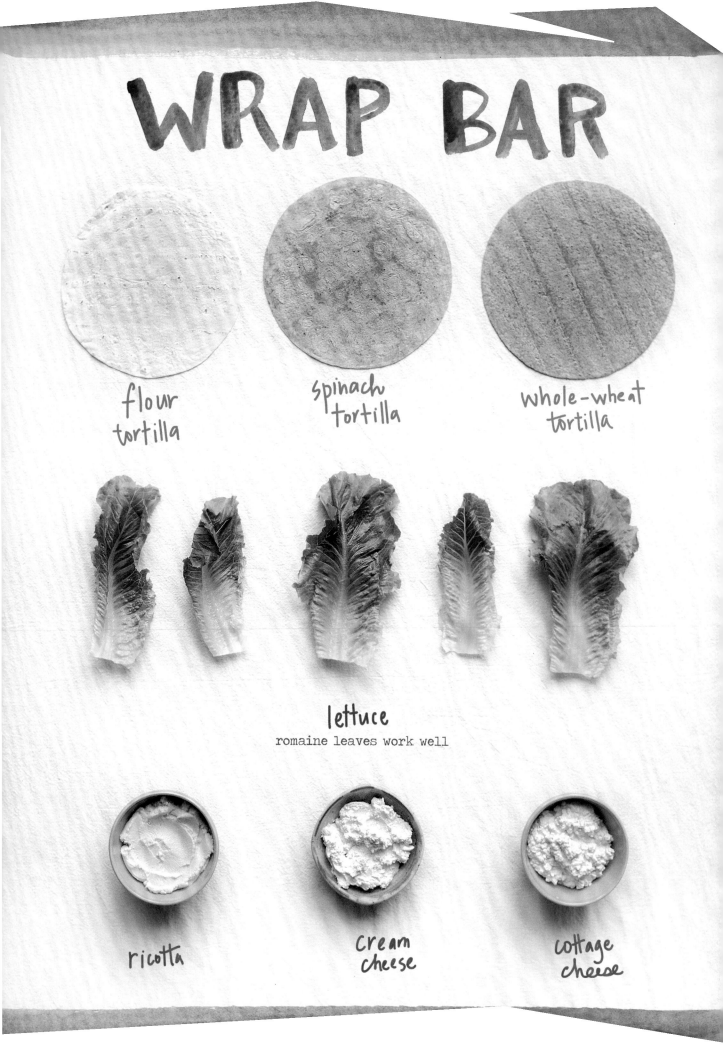

WRAP BAR

flour tortilla

spinach tortilla

whole-wheat tortilla

lettuce
romaine leaves work well

ricotta

cream cheese

cottage cheese

This menu works wonderfully as a lunch or light dinner & could also be served alongside soup. All the ingredients can be served on the buffet table at room temp. Everything except for the avocado can be prepared ahead & stored in the fridge. I also set out a couple salad dressings, olive oil, balsamic vinegar, salt & pepper. Use these ideas as a starting point & add your own toppings!

baby
spinach

grated
carrots

roasted
red peppers

edamame   hummus

marinated
tofu

I usually buy
Teriyaki flavor

lentils

any type works;
I use canned French

pepitas

shelled, salted &
roasted pumpkin seeds

avocado

slice or mash & sprinkle
with lemon or lime juice

scallions

slice the white
and green parts

favorite combinations:

cream cheese | carrots | tofu | red peppers | pepitas

cottage cheese | scallions | carrots | lentils

ricotta | hummus | spinach | pepitas | edamame

CREAMY POLENTA BAR

polenta

see opposite for cooking instructions

pesto

I use store-bought

marinara

serve warm

grated Cheddar

feta

sautéed mushrooms

slice & sauté with
olive oil, salt & pepper;
serve warm or at room temp

All of these ingredients can be prepared in advance & put out at room temperature, except for the polenta & the marinara, which should be served hot. Make the polenta right before you serve it to make sure it doesn't harden. Follow package instructions, but for 6 servings, I usually boil 12 c (2.8 L) water in a big pot then add 3 c (360 g) dry polenta & allow to simmer on low for about 5 min until thickened, stirring frequently. You can also stir in a dollop of goat cheese, Greek yogurt, butter, or grated cheese to make it creamier. Plus I always stir in a pinch of salt, pepper & garlic powder. Have a guest help you make up bowls in the kitchen to pass out, or pour the polenta into a slow-cooker to keep it warm on a buffet while guests serve themselves.

caramelized onion & leek

see page 192 for cooking instructions

sautéed red bell pepper

seed, cube & sauté with olive oil, garlic, salt & pepper; serve warm or at room temp

sautéed fresh spinach

sauté with olive oil, garlic, salt & pepper; serve warm or at room temp

cilantro

pine nuts

sunflower seeds

scallions

chop the white & green parts

BUFFET TABLE TIPS

* place some items on wooden
  boxes or stacks of cookbooks
  to give your table some height

* decorate your
  buffet with potted
  plants instead of flowers

* Keep polenta warm
  & creamy in a slow-cooker

acknowledgments

I feel so lucky that I married someone who loves throwing parties as much as I do! Thank you, Jonathan, for being the best cohost I could ever ask for. And for putting up with so many candles, mason jars, and mismatched plates in our cupboards! Thank you to my parents and brother, Mike, Steph, and Ryan, and to Jonathan's parents, Jim and Wendy, for teaching us the importance of welcoming people into our home.

Thank you to my incredible editor, Laura, who understands me and this book so perfectly and whose impeccable taste and advice I can always trust! Thank you to Sally Knapp, Liam Flanagan, Danny Maloney, and everyone at Abrams for letting me do all the parts of this crazy amazing cookbook art project my way. It's been a DREAM to work with all of you.

Thank you to my literary agent, Alison Fargis, for always knowing what I want before I say it, for unending support, and for continuing to help me grow *The Forest Feast*.

Thank you, John and Laney, for sharing Skyline with us, and thank you to the team and farmers behind our CSA, Eating with the Seasons—your produce inspires me weekly. A special thanks to Marc Lipovsky for contributing his unique and stunning aerial photographs.

Thank you to all my recipe testers, who hosted these parties and gave me invaluable feedback: Jenna Wachtel, Robert Pronovost, Anya and Ted Glenn, Julia Thibaud, Maddy Bloch, Arielle Traub, Ethan Prosnit, Jenna Weinberg, Jake Prosnit, Aaren Alpert, Adina Alpert, Talia Kravitz, Wendy Bloch, Jim Prosnit, Martha Bixby, Laura Keller, Jodie Liudhardt, Tabitha St. Bernard-Jacobs, Adam Jacobs, Stacy Ladenburger, Lauren Michele, Joe Caves, Shannon Gleeson, Gabe Carraher, Margaret Jacobs, George Rosenberg, Yasmin de la Vega, Ted De Barbieri, Kate Seely-Kirk, Bridget Schum, Marygiulia Capobianco, Stephen Jacobs, Gabrielle Langholtz, Andrea Davidson, and Jeff Malamy.

Thank you to our friends and family, who trekked all the way out to the woods for our parties, brought jackets because you knew we'd be outside, and drove the dark and winding road home. I feel truly grateful to have such a loving and supportive community around me in my daily life, and online. Thank you to the readers around the world who make my recipes and post them. Your kind comments and sweet enthusiasm inspire me to keep creating and cooking.

index